PHILIPPIANS
Rejoice in the Lord

JUAN SANCHEZ

Lifeway Press®
Brentwood, Tennessee

EDITORIAL TEAM

Cynthia Hopkins
Writer

Reid Patton
Senior Editor

Angel Prohaska
Associate Editor

Jon Rodda
Art Director

Tyler Quillet
Managing Editor

Joel Polk
Publisher, Small Group Publishing

Brian Daniel
Director, Adult Ministry Publishing

Published by Lifeway Press® • © 2023 Juan Sanchez

ISBN 978-1-0877-7828-0 • Item 005840908

Dewey decimal classification: 22.7.6
Subject headings: BIBLE. N.T. PHILIPPIANS \ JOY AND SORROW \ HAPPINESS

The structure of this study is based on the "Four Coordinates" of theology found in Michael Horton's *Pilgrim Theology*, (Grand Rapids: Zondervan, 2012.) Used with permission from the author.

To order additional copies of this resource, write to Lifeway Resources Customer Service; 200 Powell Place, Suite 100; Brentwood, TN 37027-7707; fax 615-251-5933; phone toll free 800-458-2772; order online at Lifeway.com; or email orderentry@lifeway.com.

Printed in the United States of America

Groups Ministry Publishing • Lifeway Resources • 200 Powell Place, Suite 100 • Brentwood, TN 37027-7707

CONTENTS

ABOUT
THE AUTHOR

Juan Sanchez has served as senior pastor of High Pointe Baptist Church since August 2005. He is a graduate of the University of Florida and holds an MDiv, a ThM, and a PhD in systematic theology from the Southern Baptist Theological Seminary. In addition, Juan serves as a council member of the Gospel Coalition, cofounder and president of Coalición, and associate professor of theology at Southwestern Baptist Theological Seminary. He has authored numerous books, including *1 Peter for You* and *Seven Dangers Facing your Church*. His most recent book is *The Leadership Formula: Develop the Next Generation of Leaders in the Church*. Juan has been married to Jeanine since 1990, and they have five adult daughters.

HOW TO USE THIS STUDY

This Bible study provides a guided process for individuals and small groups to find their joy in the Lord, using the book of Philippians as an entry point. Eight sessions of study examine the book of Philippians, continually pointing us back to our joy in Christ. This study is organized on a discipleship pathway of Drama, Doctrine, Doxology, and Discipleship.

GROUP STUDY

Regardless of what day of the week your group meets, each session of content begins with the group session. Each group session uses the following format to facilitate simple yet meaningful interaction among group members and with God's Word.

START

The group session will begin with a few questions designed to help you introduce the session's topic of study and encourage everyone to engage with the study.

WATCH

This space is left blank so that you can take notes during the group video teaching.

DRAMA (MAIN GROUP SESSION)

This section is the main component of the group session. The questions provided are designed to facilitate the group study of the session's topic. The goal is to better understand the story line of Scripture we find in Philippians.

PERSONAL STUDY

Three days of personal study are provided after each group session to help individuals think biblically about the session's topic. With biblical teaching and introspective questions, these lessons challenge individuals to grow in their understanding of God's Word and to respond in faith and obedience.

DOCTRINE

The group session is designed to help us understand the key text in Philippians. The Doctrine section takes this idea deeper. To do that, we need to answer the question: What key beliefs/convictions arise from this text? This first personal study will lead participants to dive deeper into the text from Philippians and related texts to develop a fuller understanding of beliefs and convictions that naturally arise from the text.

DOXOLOGY

Once we understand something true about God, we must respond to that truth with our spiritual worship (Romans 12:1). Scripture should change how we relate to God. This second personal study guides participants to see and understand what the text teaches them about God and His character and offers them direction as to how to respond. This might be a journal-like prompt, prayer, Scripture memorization, or a directed activity.

DISCIPLESHIP

Lastly, Scripture must be applied to be understood. Based on the previous days of study wrestling with the text, we must consider what substantive changes we are going to make considering what God said. This section answers the question: Where is the text leading us to act?

Session One

The Joy of
GOSPEL
PARTNERSHIPS

GROUP STUDY

START

Welcome everyone to session 1.

Ask participants to introduce themselves, including
a quick answer to the following question:

**When was the last time you clapped about something? What was it and
why did you respond that way?**

Some people express emotions often and freely, while others seek to keep their emotions in check or avoid them altogether. But rejoicing in the Lord is less about leaning into a particular personality trait or outward expression as it is about leaning into a true understanding of who God is and what He is doing in our lives. That's what Philippians is all about!

**What did you join this study hoping to learn? Or, now that you're here,
what do you hope to gain?**

In our first session, we'll examine Philippians 1:1-11. Paul's introductory words reveal the reasons for joy that he will unpack throughout the letter. They also include a prayer that expresses what Paul hoped the recipients of his letter would gain. We are also recipients of Paul's letter, so let's join in that prayer as a way of preparing to watch video session 1:

*Father, as we study Philippians, we ask that You would cause our love to keep
on growing in knowledge, so that we might rejoice in You and be pure and
blameless in the day of Christ. Let this study result in your glory and praise.*

WATCH

Use this space to take notes during the video teaching.

DRAMA

Use the following questions and prompts to guide
your discussion of the video teaching.

**Considering that Paul wrote this letter from prison, is the attitude
he expresses in Philippians 1:1-11 surprising to you? Explain.**

**Why is thankfulness to God in joyful prayer appropriate in every
circumstance (vv. 3-4)? What reasons do we have to always be
thankful to God?**

Paul was thankful to God for the joyful gift of partnership with other believers. Juan
explained that the word *partnership* in verse 5 comes from a Greek word that means
"to share or to participate in," and signifies a deep relationship of mutual love and support.
In the case of Paul's relationship with the Philippians, his "partnership" involved a financial gift, prayer, and standing firm in living out the gospel together.

**Why should our partnership with other believers consist of more than just
"hanging out"? How does gospel partnership extend beyond standard
friendship?**

**When have you experienced the kind of joy in gospel partnership that
Paul described? What caused that joy?**

**What does it look like for us to partner together in an ongoing way (v. 5)?
Why is the joy Paul described impossible in partnership that only occurs
from time to time when it's convenient?**

Read Philippians 1:6-7.

**How are gospel partnerships related to spiritual growth? How has God
used gospel partnerships to cultivate the good work He started in you?**

As we commit to ongoing partnership with other believers, God uses those relationships to deepen our faith and reveal more of Himself to us. Juan highlighted three reasons why we should rejoice in gospel partnerships:

1. It glorifies God as the generous provider of His gospel workers.
2. It allows us to participate in the Great Commission.
3. It is evidence of our salvation.

Which of these reasons for rejoicing in gospel partnerships stand out to you? Why?

Read Philippians 1:9-11.

What is the connection between our joy in gospel partnerships and our understanding ("knowledge," v. 9) of what Christ has done for us?

How should Paul's prayer for the Philippian believers inform our prayers for each other?

God gives us the gift of partnership with other believers to help meet our daily needs, propel us forward, and assure us of His presence in the gospel work He has called us to. Pursing the work and call of God with others gives us reason to rejoice in the Lord!

What remaining questions or comments do you have about this session's teaching video? What was challenging, convicting, encouraging, or timely for your current circumstances?

CLOSE IN PRAYER.

Prayer Requests:

DOCTRINE

What would you expect future readers of modern correspondence to find when looking back on the world today? Formality or informality? Emojis? GIFs? Text messages? The first-century Greco-Roman world followed formal practices when writing letters. The letter to the Philippians reflects the etiquette of the day. It also reflects Paul's particular skill in weaving theology into all parts of his correspondence, even the introduction, and leaves us a rich history of first-century believers.

Read Philippians 1:1-2. What does the greeting of this letter communicate about its author?

What does it communicate about its recipients?

What does it state about its purpose?

Sadly, too many professing Christians have a low view of the church—to the point that there are pastors and church leaders who try to make the church more relevant or exciting. This greeting to the Philippians offers a higher view. Jesus is our Lord. He is our Master. There is nothing He cannot ask of His servants. And His aim for us is that we become like Him and lead like Him, raising up even more faithful people who are committed to serving His church. The New Testament doesn't know anything of a Christian apart from a church.

Practically, what does it look like to commit to a local gathering of the saints?

Why do many people find the experience of commitment to the church unpleasant (low view) instead of joyful (high view)?

If anyone had a right to criticize the church, every church, it was the apostle Paul. And as we read through the New Testament letters, we see that he did! But, Paul didn't just criticize them, he pointed them back to Christ and to the gospel.

Read Philippians 1:3-8. What are two reasons why Paul thanked God?

The words *partnership* (v. 5) and *partners* (v. 7) come from the Greek word *koinonia*. We tend to translate this word as "fellowship," which brings to our minds hanging out, eating food, and drinking coffee. But that's not how this word is used in the New Testament. It is used to denote sharing and having something in common. Paul and the Philippians shared a deep relationship of mutual love, support, and care. And Paul thanked God for that partnership. We can thank God for that kind of partnership, too! When you came to faith in Christ, we all became partners in the same gospel.

How does commonality enhance friendship and commitment?

In what ways are all believers called to live out the partnership of the gospel?

- ☐ financial giving
- ☐ prayer
- ☐ time
- ☐ resources
- ☐ missions
- ☐ sharing the gospel
- ☐ personal discipleship
- ☐ pursuing holiness

Read 1 John 3:16-18. What might it say about us if we do not partner together in the ways noted above?

Some days you don't feel like you can be generous with your time and resources. Some days you miss opportunities to share the gospel and fail to pray like you should. Other believers fail, too. But we can still be thankful to God for inviting us into partnership with His church. Because God is at work in us, He will finish that work! Salvation is a process; it does not lead to instant perfection. Paul was confident about that, and we can be, too.

||| *God works in us to produce works that bring Him glory.* |||

How does confidence in the Lord's saving work in His church impact your view of gospel partnership?

How does knowing that God's work is more dependent on Him than on us change the way you think about gospel partnership?

In addition to partnership with fellow believers, our ultimate partnership is with God. He will begin and finish the work He desires. He is more than able. One of the ways He works is through the partnership in the church. We can give thanks to God for the church because of our partnership in the gospel and our confidence in the Lord's saving work among us. Through Jesus we have a shared work and common goal to take the gospel to the ends of the earth.

Read Philippians 1:9-11. In your own words, what did Paul pray for the church?

Since Paul was joyful about the Philippians' gospel partnership and confident that God would complete His saving work among them (vv. 3-6), why did he feel the need to pray for their spiritual growth?

Why should we pray for even those things we feel most confident that God will accomplish?

The Philippian church was loving. Still, the unity of that church, like every church, was threatened by opposition (1:27), personal conflicts (2:14; 4:2-3), false teachers (3:2-3), and worldliness (3:17-19). So, Paul prayed that their love would grow more and more, with knowledge and discernment. That is because love without knowledge and discernment, or truth, is just sentimentalism.

How does the world define love based on sentimentalism? Give an example.

Christian love—both for God and others—stands in contrast to the sentimental love of the world. Growth in the knowledge of God leads to discernment and Christian maturity that presents itself through love. Christian maturity is rooted in knowledge and love. Knowledge or truth without love is not spiritual maturity at all—it is proud and leads to legalism. True spiritual maturity seeks to apply the knowledge of God to every situation, in love.

Reread verse 10. Why do believers need to pray for each other to grow in knowledge and discernment?

What does it mean to "approve the things that are superior"?

Life is a series of choices, and we choose what we love the most. We make life choices and relational choices based on what we love and what we know. As Christians, we are to choose what is excellent—what is of more value and superior—based on what we have learned about God—His Word, His purposes, and His ways. This is what the Bible calls wisdom.

For what reason did Paul want his gospel partners to choose the things that are superior?

What is the result (vv. 10-11)?

How are God and other believers helping you accomplish this goal?

Jesus is coming again to judge the living and the dead. When He returns, each of us will give an account for the choices we made, whether poor or excellent. Our lives will serve as evidence. So we pray that, on that day, our lives will have produced a harvest of righteousness—not for our glory, but for the glory of God.

> *In light of the second coming, let us pray that we may grow in discerning love, so as to choose what is excellent, in order to be found blameless on the day of Christ.*

DOXOLOGY

WRITE IT DOWN

How have you experienced the joy of partnership in the church? Use the space below to write a prayer of thanks to God.

HIDE IT IN YOUR HEART

One way to grow in joyful, gospel partnership and maturity is to not just read God's Word, but to store God's Word in our hearts (Psalm 119:11). This week, memorize Philippians 1:9-11. As you do, begin praying that prayer for yourself and other believers.

> *And I pray this: that your love will keep on growing in knowledge and every kind of discernment, so that you may approve the things that are superior and may be pure and blameless in the day of Christ, filled with the fruit of righteousness that comes through Jesus Christ to the glory and praise of God.*

PHILIPPIANS 1:9-11

DISCIPLESHIP

Now that you've expressed thanks to God for the joy of partnership in His church, consider the reasons you are sometimes more critical than thankful.

Consider your view of gospel partnerships in the church. Where do you need to invite the Lord to correct your thoughts towards the church? What is your responsibility in that process?

What steps do you need to take so that your love will keep on growing in knowledge and every kind of discernment?

Being thankful for the church doesn't always come naturally. How can you be on the lookout for evidences of God's saving grace in other people's lives?

What would it look like, practically, for you to choose what is superior this week?

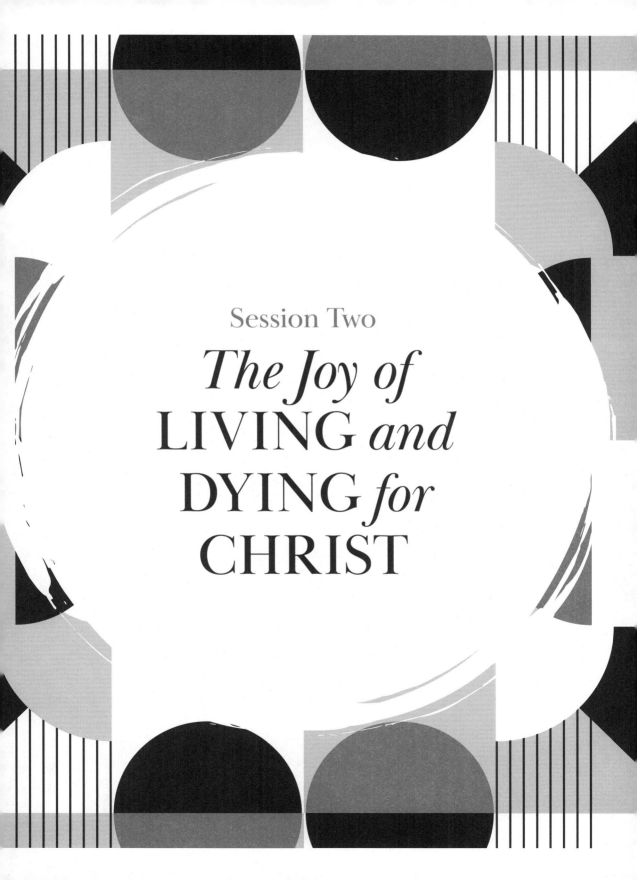

Session Two

The Joy of LIVING *and* DYING *for* CHRIST

GROUP STUDY

START

Welcome everyone to the group. Take a few minutes to
review session 1 before starting session 2.

Before starting the new content each week, we'll take a few minutes to review the personal study from the previous week. The review questions will focus on three general themes: doctrine—what beliefs naturally arise from the biblical text, doxology—how to respond to what the text teaches you about God, and discipleship—what changes you are going to make as you consider what God said.

DOCTRINE. What is one key belief/conviction that arose from the text?

DOXOLOGY. What is one way you can respond to that belief/conviction in worship?

DISCIPLESHIP. How is the text leading you to act differently going forward?

Reviewing the previous week's study serves two essential purposes:
1. Review sets the context for the drama (story) we're about to study and discuss in Scripture.
2. Review provides accountability for doxology and discipleship—putting into practice the things we're learning about God and about ourselves.

Throughout Paul's letter to the Philippians, we discover the joy we can experience and demonstrate as we lean into a true understanding of who God is and what He is doing in our lives. This week we're going to examine the joy of living and dying for Christ.

To prepare for video session 2, pray that God will help
each person understand and apply this truth:

*When what drives us is the glory of God in Jesus Christ,
we can rejoice—no matter what circumstances we face.*

WATCH

Use this space to take notes during the video teaching.

DRAMA

Use the following questions and prompts to guide
your discussion of the video teaching.

Can you relate to Juan's analogy of living a roller coaster life, where your joy goes up and down based on circumstances? Explain.

Why do so many of us tend to live this way?

Read Philippians 1:12-20.

Through what lens did Paul view every circumstance of his life?

In what situation in your life do you need to adopt the attitude, "What does it matter? Only that in every way . . . Christ is proclaimed, and in this I rejoice" (v. 18)?

We tend to equate joy with good things we accomplish or good things that happen to us— a promotion, a new relationship, a fun vacation, a long-awaited purchase, a healthy bank account. Most of us consider these good personal circumstances as "wins" that serve as the basis of our joy. But true joy is less circumstantial.

Do you think most believers regularly consider the proclamation of Christ as a personal "win" and reason for joy? Why should we?

Based on verse 19, what helps us move from a circumstance-based joy (emotional roller coaster) to a steady joy that is rooted in Christ alone? What is your role in stepping into that growth process?

Read Philippians 1:21-30.

Considering that Paul faced the very real possibility of being killed for his faith, why didn't he ask the Philippians to pray for his physical safety? How did the foundation of joy in Christ impact Paul's view of death?

In the teaching video, Juan pointed out that Paul was in a "no-lose situation" (v. 21). He didn't base his "wins" on good personal circumstances; he based them on the life of Christ in him—which he knew to be an eternal truth. So if he was executed, it was a win. If he lived, it was a win. Even in his imprisonment, Paul continued to speak of Jesus in front of Caesar and anyone else.

Do you currently view both life and death as reasons for joy? Why?

Based on verses 27-30, what challenge is there for Christians today? How can this group pray for you in that?

What remaining questions or comments do you have about this session's teaching video? What was challenging, convicting, encouraging, or timely for your current circumstances?

CLOSE IN PRAYER.

Prayer Requests:

DOCTRINE

The blessing of gospel partnership with other believers wasn't the only joy in Paul's life. He didn't experience trouble and then think, "My life is so hard, but at least I have good friends!" No, Paul found reason for joy even *in* his troubles, and he was familiar with difficult circumstances.

Read Philippians 1:12-13. What happened because of Paul's imprisonment?

Based on these verses, how would you describe Paul's worldview?

Paul was not looking back on a hard time in his life with sudden insight about what God had done. He wrote the letter to the Philippians *from prison*. Difficult circumstances were still upon him, and there was no solution in sight. Yet Paul didn't complain about it. He understood that his imprisonment was not outside God's sovereign control, and rejoiced because his imprisonment advanced the gospel. Paul's animating purpose was the spread of the glory of God in Christ. His mission did not change based on his circumstance. He would preach the gospel of the Jewish Messiah to Gentiles wherever God placed him.

Why do many Christians today continually pursue and prioritize temporary circumstances as having ultimate importance in our lives?

We should be driven to spread the glory of God in Jesus Christ.

Read Philippians 1:14-19. It wasn't Paul's words and actions alone that made a gospel impact in his circumstance. What else happened?

Notice that Paul used the word *brothers* in verse 14, not *elders* or *pastors*. Does it seem strange to you that Paul did not rely only on church leaders to proclaim the gospel? Why?

Paul's imprisonment gave courage to other Christians to proclaim Christ more boldly. The advance of the gospel is the responsibility of the church, "the brothers." Jesus commanded us to advance the gospel (Matthew 28:19-20). And Jesus promised us that the gospel *will* advance (Matthew 16:15-18). So, even in our fears and difficulties, we can be encouraged to proclaim Christ in whatever circumstances we find ourselves. The faithful proclamation of Christ advances the gospel—whether or not people immediately repent and believe.

From what you learn in verses 15-17, why might Paul have complained about the brothers?

Does verse 18 mean we should not be bothered whether or not we and others pursue right motives in ministry? What does it mean?

Evidently, some believers were jealous of Paul and took advantage of his imprisonment to advance their own ministries—in opposition to Paul's. Sadly, we see similar kinds of impure motives in Christian ministry today. Certainly this self-serving behavior would have grieved Paul. To be sure, he was not saying that motives do not matter. But he understood that because God is sovereign, even impure, sinful motives cannot hinder the gospel's advance. God would be glorified, the Philippians would pray, the Holy Spirit would help, and, ultimately, Paul would be vindicated (v. 19). In this, Paul could rejoice. And we should rejoice.

||| *We can rejoice whenever and wherever Christ is proclaimed, because when Christ is preached, the gospel advances.* |||

Read Philippians 1:20-26. What was Paul's eager expectation and hope?

What joy did Paul have in living through every circumstance he encountered?

Because of his imprisonment and trial, death was an ever-present possibility for Paul. Why was he joyful even when considering the possibility of dying an early and unjust death?

Paul fully expected because of the prayers of the Philippians and the help of the Holy Spirit (v. 19) that he would not deny Christ before Caesar. Instead, he would have the courage to boldly proclaim Christ, whether by life or by death—faithful witness in prison and before Caesar or faithful martyrdom at the hands of Caesar.

Read Ephesians 2:8-9. What was Paul's confidence regarding his future vindication before God on the last day?

☐ **being courageous before Caesar**	☐ **leading people to Christ**	☐ **going on mission trips**
☐ **his service to the churches**	☐ **turning his life around**	☐ **being a good leader**
☐ **selflessness**	☐ **enduring prison**	☐ **Christ alone**

Joy-filled confidence for vindication on the last day is found in Christ alone. There is nothing any of us can do to save ourselves. And there is nothing any of us have done that Jesus cannot forgive. Paul was a blasphemer and a murderer. By his own testimony, he was the worst of sinners (1 Timothy 1:15). And he trusted in Christ alone for his present vindication and justification before God. Not only that, but he continued trusting in Christ alone for his future vindication before God on the last day.

Based on Philippians 1:25-26, how should a person's confidence in future vindication in Christ alone impact his or her life in the present? One example is given. List a few more.

1. *He or she would make financial decisions based on what would most exalt Christ and help others know Christ.*

2.

3.

4.

Paul's focus was not the glory of self—it was the glory of God in Jesus Christ. His focus was not the progress of self—it was the progress of the gospel. His focus was not avoiding temporary displeasures—it was realizing eternal treasures. So he was willing to continue to suffer if the gospel would advance through him. Part of that gospel advancement would take place as the Philippians followed Paul's example. It also takes place as we, today, follow that same example.

> *When the glory of God in Christ is what drives us, our singular focus will be on the progress of others in their faith and joy.*

Read Philippians 1:27-30. What impact should living for the glory of God in Jesus Christ have on the community of faith?

What is the purpose of the church? How does disunity hurt that purpose?

The believers in Philippi faced difficulties, too, and Paul wanted them to be ready to face those difficulties with the glory of God in Christ as their primary focus. To do that—to live life worthy of the gospel—they would need each other. While God offers each of us salvation as individuals, we must live out our salvation in the context of community. Working for the advancement of the gospel is a cooperative venture, requiring team effort. As we live out our faith for all to see, we are to be of one mind, focused together on the call of the gospel. In fact, living our lives in a manner worthy of the gospel requires this kind of unity of faith, calling, and purpose.

Why did Paul infer that adversity is a privilege? How might adversity help us to refocus our lives on eternal matters?

Paul reminded the believers in Philippi that their struggles meant neither that God was punishing them nor that He was abandoning them. Rather, using the analogy of athletic contests, he showed that our struggling or striving for the gospel gives us assurance that we are in the game. Furthermore, through our struggles we have opportunities to encourage one another as believers as we together give our lives for the cause of the gospel.

> *The pursuit of the glory of God in Christ is joyfully lived out in the context of the unified community of faith.*

DOXOLOGY

WRITE IT DOWN

Why do you wake up in the morning? What drives you? What excites you? In the space below, make a list of those things.

CALL UPON GOD

As you acknowledge any eternally meaningless priorities in your life, ask God to change your perspective. Ask Him to wake you up each and every morning with the drive to advance the gospel, no matter what circumstance you may find yourself in that day, so that He would be glorified in His Son, Jesus Christ.

HIDE IT IN YOUR HEART

As a help for developing a singular focus on the glory of God in Christ Jesus, memorize Philippians 1:20. To help with that, consider writing it on a notecard and placing it in a location you regularly look.

My eager expectation and hope is that I will not be ashamed about anything, but that now as always, with all courage, Christ will be highly honored in my body, whether by life or by death.

PHILIPPIANS 1:20

DISCIPLESHIP

What are you relying on for your future vindication before God? How do you know?

What changes would take place in your life if what drove you each day was the spread of the glory of God in Christ? What steps do you need to take to make those changes?

What does unity in the community of faith have to do with living your life worthy of the gospel? Do you usually put the two together as one? Why or why not?

How might you encourage other believers to live lives worthy of the gospel this week?

Session Three

The Joy of
HUMILITY

GROUP STUDY

START

Welcome everyone to the group. Take a few minutes to
review session 2 before starting session 3.

Before starting the new content each week, we'll take a few minutes to review the personal study from the previous week. The review questions will focus on three general themes: doctrine—what beliefs naturally arise from the biblical text, doxology—how to respond to what the text teaches you about God, and discipleship—what changes you are going to make as you consider what God said.

DOCTRINE. What is one key belief/conviction that arose from the text?

DOXOLOGY. What is one way you can respond to that belief/conviction in worship?

DISCIPLESHIP. How is the text leading you to act differently going forward?

The joy of living and dying for Christ is largely an effect of relational community. In Christ, Paul's earthly life gave him joy because it gave him opportunities to minister to other people. His death, too, would be a testimony of the gospel. However, those effects are not automatic for any of us. To impart and receive the joy God intends, this week we'll discuss the way to make the most of those earthly relationships by embracing Christlike humility.

To prepare for video session 3, pray that God will help
each person understand and apply this truth:

||| *The key to humility is having the mindset of Christ.* |||

WATCH

Use this space to take notes during the video teaching.

DRAMA

Use the following questions and prompts to guide
your discussion of the video teaching.

To start this week's video teaching, Juan related church life to family life and said, "Family life is fun but family life is also messy." Why is this true? Why is this important for members of any local church to understand?

In your own experience, have you felt the tension in church life between fun and messy? How so? How do you tend to navigate those two realities?

Read John 17:20-21.

What is challenging for us in Jesus's prayer here?

Is it possible for church life to be messy and unified at the same time? How?

Philippians 1 ends by making the point that if we treasure the gospel we will stand firm against external opponents (vv. 27-30). Paul continues the teaching in chapter 2, reasoning that if we treasure the gospel we will also stand firm against internal divisions. After all, we cannot possibly stand firm together against external opponents if we are not standing together in the unity of Christ. And, as Jesus made clear in John 17, Christian unity has extraordinary and eternally significant effects.

Read Philippians 2:1-4.

Juan described a strong form of pride ("Look at me!") and a weak form of pride ("Woe is me"). Each of us battles pride, and both forms can be subtle and easily missed. What steps can we take to recognize the pride within us as we relate to each other in the life of the church?

Read Philippians 2:5-8.

In understanding Christ's attitude, what phrases in verses 6-8 stand out to you today as especially revealing?

What does it look like, practically, for believers to take on Christ's attitude? Give an example from contemporary church life.

Read Philippians 2:9-11 and the point Juan drew from it:
We not only follow Jesus's footsteps into suffering and death,
we follow Jesus's footsteps into resurrection and glory.

Why should the promise of future glory impact the reality of present conflicts?

What changes would occur in our lives if we took on the mindset of Jesus Christ? What changes would occur in our church? What changes would occur in the global church? What effect would those changes bring?

How can this group pray for you in your need to take on the mindset of Christ so that you might grow in and experience the joy of humility?

What remaining questions or comments do you have about this session's teaching video? What was challenging, convicting, encouraging, or timely for your current circumstances?

CLOSE IN PRAYER.

Prayer Requests:

DOCTRINE

In the first chapter of Philippians, we learned that there is joy in gospel partnerships and also in living and dying for Christ. Paul continued expressing his joy in Christ and desire to share that joy with others in chapter 2. After exhorting the Philippians believers to live their lives "worthy of the gospel of Christ," "standing firm in one spirit, in one accord," all while struggling in suffering (1:27-30), Paul told them how.

Read Philippians 2:1-4. What four instructions did Paul give in verse 2?

Which of these stands out to you as especially difficult in the community of faith? Why?

The ground for Paul's appeal for Christian unity is the salvation we experience in union with Christ. All who have been united with Christ by faith have His encouragement, consolation, fellowship, affection, and mercy (v. 1). Those blessings necessitate that we share with one another what God has shared with us in Christ. Relationships are hard. Brothers and sisters in Christ will disagree, but unity is essential.

Read John 13:34-35 and Romans 15:5-6. Why is unity among believers such a big deal?

We must keep growing. In our flesh and in this world, pride will always threaten our unity.

There are numerous Scripture passages about the need for unity among God's people. Numerous passages also detail *disunity* among God's people.

Complete the following chart to see why Christian unity matters.

Scripture	Prideful Problem	What message this disunity would have given to outsiders
Acts 5:1-4		
Romans 14:13-18		
1 Corinthians 1:11-17		
Revelation 2:4-5		
Revelation 2:20		
Revelation 3:1-2		
Revelation 3:15-17		

We all battle the sin of pride, and we need to admit it, confess it, and repent of it because it does great damage. Pride produces divisions and conflict, destroys unity, and compromises our witness. Unity in Christ, on the other hand, produces joy (Philippians 2:2)! If we're to live in the same mindset that produces that joy-filled unity, we need to adopt Jesus's mindset.

Read Philippians 2:5. How does it strike you to read this as a command?

Is it fair or reasonable to command a Christlike attitude in the life of every believer, even those who never had any earthly examples of genuine humility to go by? Why?

> *The key to Christian unity is sharing the mindset of Christ in His incarnation.*

Sharing the mindset of Christ is both a gift of our union with Him—"which is yours in Christ Jesus" (ESV), and it is our responsibility to cultivate it—"Adopt the same attitude as that of Christ Jesus" (CSB).

How would you explain what it means to have the mindset of Christ?

Read Philippians 2:6-8. How does Paul describe Christ's attitude? Mark every word that applies.

☐ selfless   ☐ humble   ☐ obedient
☐ selfish   ☐ prideful   ☐ disobedient

Why was it an act of selflessness for Christ to "[assume] the form of a servant"?

Why was it an act of humility for Christ to "[take] on the likeness of humanity" (v. 7)?

Why was it an act of obedience for Christ to face "death on a cross" (v. 8)?

Jesus, God the Son, selflessly set aside His divine glory and status, humbled Himself by becoming a man, and obeyed the Father all the way to the cross—the most humiliating death of that time. And if you are a Christian, you are united with Christ—in His suffering, burial, and death.

What does it look like when Christians follow in the steps of Jesus and adopt the mindset of selflessness? Give an example.

What does it look like when Christians follow in the steps of Jesus and adopt the mindset of humility? Give an example.

What does it look like when Christians follow in the steps of Jesus and adopt the mindset of obedience? Give an example.

Most people don't consider selflessness, humility, and obedience as the pathway to joy. Rather, they think the way to find joy is to prioritize the needs and desires of self. Even believers are prone to think this way.

In Christ, cultivating selflessness, humility, and obedience brings joy. Why?

Read Philippians 2:9-11. How did God the Father respond to Jesus's selflessness, humility, and obedience?

What future promise of worldwide selflessness, humility, and obedience do these verses give? How should this impact our present mindset?

What insight do the following verses add to your understanding of Philippians 2:9-11?

Romans 8:16-17

2 Timothy 2:11

The result of our union with Christ is that we are not only united with Him in His suffering and death, but also in His resurrection and exaltation.

DOXOLOGY

WRITE IT DOWN, CALL UPON GOD, AND HIDE IT IN YOUR HEART

Peter and James were two guys who struggled with Christ's call to humility. Peter was brash and outspoken. He cut off a man's ear. He had a big mouth and carried a big sword—and he was quick to use both. But Peter was committed to Jesus in the process of ongoing spiritual growth. As a result, a huge transformation took place in his life.

James had a similar personality, only he was one of Jesus's actual brothers. But James didn't look up to Jesus and idolize Him like some little brothers do. In fact, James didn't believe that Jesus was the Messiah until after He died and rose again. He even challenged Jesus to show Himself to the world. Why? Because humility is often most difficult with your family and the people you're closest to.

1. In the passages below, read what Peter wrote and what scholars think Jesus's brother James likely wrote after Jesus died, rose, ascended to heaven, and sent His Holy Spirit.
2. The struggle between humility and pride is a spiritual battle. Record what Peter and James wanted you to learn from their experiences.
3. Write a prayer inviting God to transform your attitude, too.
4. Choose one of the two passages to memorize.

1 Peter 5:6-8

James 4:6-10

Prayer:

DISCIPLESHIP

In what situation or relationship do you need to adopt Christ's attitude of humility?

Since humility is both a gift of your union with Christ and a responsibility of yours to cultivate, how will that transformation take place? How will you participate in the process?

Review the chart on page 44. Is there any way you are contributing to disunity in the body of Christ—in purpose, attitude, words, or practice? What do you need to do about it?

Name one practical way you could selflessly humble yourself in obedience to help other believers develop greater unity this week.

Session Four

The Joy of
OBEDIENCE

GROUP STUDY

START

Welcome everyone to the group. Take a few minutes to
review session 3 before starting session 4.

Before starting the new content each week, we'll take a few minutes to review the personal study from the previous week.

DOCTRINE. What is one key belief/conviction that arose from the text?

DOXOLOGY. What is one way you can respond to that belief/conviction in worship?

DISCIPLESHIP. How is the text leading you to act differently going forward?

Jesus's selfless humility compelled His full obedience to the Father's will, even to the point of death on a cross. We are also called to fully obey the Father's will, and that kind of obedience will always be connected to our humility before Him. It will always produce joy.

Share a time when pride or humility impacted your obedience to God.

To prepare for video session 4, pray that God will help
each person understand and apply this truth:

*We work to produce the fruit of our salvation
because God is working in us.*

WATCH

Use this space to take notes during the video teaching.

DRAMA

Use the following questions and prompts to guide
your discussion of the video teaching.

What are some wrong ideas people have about obedience to God's commands?

What is one word you would use to describe the attitude of your life towards obeying God's commands: joy, duty, expectation, dull, difficult, easy, circumstantial, or other? Explain.

Read Philippians 2:12-13.

Why should obedience to the Lord be a joyful endeavor?

Read Philippians 1:27 again. What clarity does "Live your life worthy of the gospel of Christ" give to the call to obedience in Philippians 2:12-13?

What are some of the works of salvation that God is calling us to produce?

What "good purpose" is God accomplishing through the obedience of His children? Why should it energize us to participate in this work?

God certainly gives us His commands for our own good, but His will for our obedience extends far beyond us. We are ambassadors for Christ (2 Corinthians 5:20). In the video teaching, Juan carried out that analogy, saying, "The church is an embassy of heaven. When the world looks at the church of Jesus Christ they're actually seeing a slice of heaven. We are showing an unbelieving world what it is like to live under the laws of King Jesus. Our obedience is connected to our witness."

When has someone else's obedience brought you joy in Christ?

How might your own obedience help someone else work out their own salvation? Give an example.

God created us for good works (Ephesians 2:10) and gives us the power to continue to produce those good works (Philippians 4:13). So what is our role in that process of working out our own salvation here on this earth?

Juan highlighted three ways the text answers that question.
1. We are to work out our own salvation in light of the last day in fear and trembling.
2. We are to work out our own salvation in wholehearted obedience.
3. We are to work out our own salvation in total dependence.

Think of an act of obedience you need to "work out." Which of these three encouragements stand out to you most personally in that struggle? Explain.

How might the daily acknowledgment that God is sovereign and at work in our lives be of benefit to us in working out our own salvation?

What remaining questions or comments do you have about this session's teaching video? What was challenging, convicting, encouraging, or timely for your current circumstances?

CLOSE IN PRAYER.

Prayer Requests:

DOCTRINE

Paul wanted to commend the Philippians to "adopt the same attitude as that of Christ Jesus" (2:5). True followers of Jesus Christ do the will of the Father. This obedience is not a means to produce salvation. Salvation is entirely dependent on the work of Jesus on the cross. Obedience is a process of learning to continually produce works that are consistent with the salvation we have received.

Read Philippians 2:12-18. Based on verses 12-13, what was Paul concerned believers might grumble and argue about (v. 14)?

The commands in verses 14-15 call to mind the people of Israel after they were redeemed from slavery in Egypt. They were God's set apart citizens in the world. God had powerfully and miraculously saved them from slavery in Egypt and made them His people. Yet in spite of that redemption, they quickly descended into grumbling and self-pity.

Read the following verses and record how Israel responded to the call to work out the salvation they so clearly had been given by God.

Exodus 16:2-3

Exodus 17:1-3

Read Exodus 16:8. What was their grumbling and arguing really all about?

How should knowing the Lord hears our grumbling affect our willingness to do so?

> *If we are to live on this earth as heavenly citizens in a manner worthy of the gospel, we must do the works that show our salvation with joy-filled contentment.*

Read 1 Peter 2:22-24 and contrast Israel's response to obedience with Christ's response.

Because God is in control, there's a sense in which all grumbling is grumbling against God. Yet when Jesus faced the most horific circumstances imaginable, He did not grumble. Jesus experienced the disappointment of betrayal and denial by His closest friends and followers. The hardship of poverty and hunger. Suffering and death at the hands of governing authorities and even His own people. And through it all, He did not grumble or argue. His circumstances were not joyful, but there was joy in His circumstance, because He followed the Father in full obedience. There is joy in obedience for us, too—even in our disappointments, hardship, and suffering.

Reread Philippians 2:16 is the key. How can we face disappointment, hardship, and suffering with joy-filled contentment?

Think back to the example of Israel as they grumbled and argued in Exodus. What were they holding onto? Mark all that apply.

- ☐ earthly comfort
- ☐ a way of life they had grown accustomed to
- ☐ an expectation of prosperity
- ☐ the Word of life
- ☐ human reasoning
- ☐ human abilities and leadership
- ☐ self-gratification

How do similar circumstances lead you into grumbling?

How might they have responded in those difficulties if they had held onto the Word of life?

The things of this world are passing away, so we should hold onto them loosely. As we release our grip on those things, we intentionally choose to hold tightly to things that have eternal value, instead—the Word that gives eternal life. The Word that saved us is the Word that sustains us. The Word anchors us and gives us joy in the storms of life. So how do we do that? What does it look like to hold onto the Word of life as we face disappointments that tempt us to grumble and argue?

Read Romans 8:26-39 and note the implications below.

PRAY, even when you don't have words (Romans 8:26-27).

REMEMBER God's goodness (Romans 8:28).

REMEMBER God's sovereignty (Romans 8:29-30).

REMEMBER God's faithfulness (Romans 8:31-36).

ENTRUST yourself to the sovereign, good, and faithful God (Romans 8:37-39).

What needs to take place in advance of disappointments in life for a person to readily remember God's goodness, sovereignty, and faithfulness in those times?

We cannot survive in this crooked and twisted world if we don't hold fast to the Word that gives life.

Reread Philippians 2:15-16. Who, besides you, is impacted when you hold onto the Word of life?

How is the unbelieving, dark world impacted when you hold onto the Word of life? Cite examples.

How are men and women God has called to be spiritual leaders impacted when you hold onto the Word of life?

We are to follow the Lord in obedience with joy-filled contentment so that the watching, unbelieving world may not lay accusations against us. Our joy in holy obedience displays the light of God's kingdom in this dark world. Further, our joy in holy obedience serves to encourage those who have obeyed God in service to us and vindicates their ministry on the last day. In other words, God takes your joy-filled obedience and multiplies its effects in ways you may never see or know.

In verses 17-18, Paul called attention to this joy of pouring out your life for the sake of others' faith, and the joy of knowing people who pour out their lives so that others might come to faith. We have the opportunity to do this today.

In what way was Paul sacrificially pouring out his life for others' faith?

What does it look like for believers to pour out their lives for the sake of others' faith?

In the Old Testament system of sacrifice, the drink offering was a secondary offering, poured over the main offering. Paul's use of that analogy in this context (v. 17) means that he didn't view his ministry, his leadership, as the main sacrifice. The ministry of the Philippians was the main sacrifice. Paul's ministry supplemented and complemented theirs. So he would be faithfully present. Even if his earthly life ended because of his obedience, he would rejoice. because his primary goal was to follow Jesus and make disciples.

Read Philippians 2:19-30. How do Paul's intentions and actions in these verses further describe his commitment to that primary goal?

What additional examples of joy-filled obedience do you find in these verses?

Both Timothy and Epaphroditus had proven themselves to be humble and selfless Christ followers, seeking to fully obey the Lord and serve people with joy. They, like Paul, were willing to sacrifice themselves for the sake of the gospel. Paul wanted the Philippians to receive servants like Timothy and Epaphroditus, so that their joy might increase.

What does it look like, practically, for believers to receive and honor faithful servants the Lord sends?

Our own joy-filled obedience grows when we receive and honor faithful servants whom the Lord sends to us.

DOXOLOGY

WRITE IT DOWN AND CALL UPON GOD

Read Romans 8:26-39 again and note the ways that passage teaches you to hold fast to the Word of life as you face disappointment, hardship, and suffering (page 59). Now prayerfully take those steps in your own life.

Confess to God a situation in which you are tempted to grumble and argue.

Remember God's goodness. List examples, even if you don't feel it right now.

Remember God's sovereignty. Write down what you know is true about God's power and rule, even if you don't understand your circumstances.

Remember God's faithfulness. Name His promises that will not fail, even when people do.

Entrust yourself to Him, committing to obey Him fully as He leads you in that circumstance.

DISCIPLESHIP

Based on your study in Philippians 2, what do you need to do to work out your own salvation?

The Israelites in Exodus grumbled because they were holding onto the things of this world, like human leadership and a way of life. Now think about your own grumbling and arguing. What are you holding onto in those moments when you resist joyful obedience to the Lord?

In what relationship or situation do you need to "shine like stars in the world"? What faithful steps of obedience can you take to do so?

Are you holding tightly to the Word of life? Are you receiving and honoring faithful servants God has sent you? What changes do you need to make to improve in those two areas?

Session Five

The Joy of
KNOWING
CHRIST

GROUP STUDY

START

Welcome everyone to the group. Take a few minutes to
review session 4 before starting session 5.

Before starting the new content each week, we'll take a few minutes to review the personal study from the previous week.

DOCTRINE. What is one key belief/conviction that arose from the text?

DOXOLOGY. What is one way you can respond to that belief/conviction in worship?

DISCIPLESHIP. How is the text leading you to act differently going forward?

We have seen in the first two chapters of Philippians the joy we can experience and demonstrate as we lean into who God is and what He is doing in our lives. While many philosophies and belief systems claim to lead to God, only the way of Jesus delivers on its claims. The clearest and most ultimate way God has shown us who He is and what He is doing in our lives is through His Son Jesus. This week we're going to examine the joy of knowing Christ.

To prepare for video session 5, pray that God will help
each person understand and apply this truth:

*We safeguard our hearts from false teachers and false
teachings by rooting our joy in the Lord Jesus Christ.*

WATCH

Use this space to take notes during the video teaching.

DRAMA

Use the following questions and prompts to guide
your discussion of the video teaching.

When did you first learn about Jesus? Where did your knowledge of Jesus primarily come from? How has your knowledge of Jesus grown?

How has knowing Jesus brought joy to your life? Give an example.

Juan described false teaching in two polar opposites—"The Gospel Plus" (legalism, adding works to attain righteousness) or "The Gospel Minus" (lawlessness, you can live however you want and still be saved).

When have you battled these tendencies in your relationship with God?

Read Philippians 3:1-11.

Has the phrase "rejoice in the Lord" ever seemed like a cliché to you? How does Philippians 3:1-11 change your understanding of the necessity of the joy of Christ in your life?

In verse 3 Paul referred to false teachers as those who "put confidence in the flesh." Where do we see this same false teaching today? Why is it important to identify anything that adds to or subtracts from the gospel as false?

From the passage, Juan drew three ways we can rejoice in the Lord in such a way that we safeguard ourselves from false teaching:

1. Remember who we are in Christ.
2. Worship God.
3. Put our confidence in Christ.

Which of those three do you struggle to embrace consistently? Why?

What are some uncertainties or doubts about who we are in Christ that are related to false teachings we have unwittingly believed?

Why do we need to remember who we are in Christ? What are some practical ways we can do that?

What pursuits do you tend to emphasize in your life that strip your focus from Christ (v. 8)?

The abundance of false teaching in the world is nothing new. It will continue to exist until Jesus returns. But we can guard our hearts from it by rooting our joy in Christ alone. When we make it our aim, like Paul, to know Christ and the power of His resurrection, to share in His suffering and death, and to look forward to the resurrection we will receive in Him, we will reject false teachings and rejoice in truth.

What remaining questions or comments do you have about this session's teaching video? What was challenging, convicting, encouraging, or timely for your current circumstances?

CLOSE IN PRAYER.

Prayer Requests:

DOCTRINE

Joy is a priority for most people, and as we have been discovering in Paul's letter to the Philippians, joy is a priority of the Christian life. However, the worldy pursuit of joy and joy in Christ manifest very differently. We honor most whatever delights us the most, and that honor displays itself in our thoughts, words, and deeds.

Read Philippians 3:1. What is the difference between the joy of the gospel and the kind of "joy" the world pursues?

When Jesus is of highest worth and value, then we enjoy Him above all other things. If we aren't finding joy in Christ, then we aren't truly worshiping God. Our joy in Christ—which can exist in any type of circumstance—should transcend all other delights in this life.

Look back at Philippians 1:4,11,18, and 25; and 2:2,14,18, and 28-29. Considering all Paul had already written on the subject, why did he emphasize the necessity of rejoicing again in Philippians 3:1?

Read Philippians 3:2-6. What danger to the Philippians' joyfulness did Paul call to their attention?

We need to hear this command over and over and over again—rejoice in the Lord!

On a scale of one to ten, how seriously does verse 2 indicate believers should take the threat of false teachers?

1   2   3   4   5   6   7   8   9   10

What would it look like for believers to take the threat of false teachers and their teachings as seriously as Philippians 3:2 commands?

What happens when we don't?

> *False teachers do the same evil work the serpent did in the garden, encouraging us to question God's Word and doubt His goodness.*

Read Genesis 3:1-7. How did Satan lead Eve to question God's words and doubt His goodness?

What competing promise of joy did Satan offer Eve?

Satan wants us to separate God's law from God's character. He uses false teachers to accomplish that. He has used this scheme since the very beginning. Satan knows that when we question God's Word and doubt His goodness, we become discontent. When we are discontent, we grumble and complain against God and His people. Once we are discontent, false teachers, like the serpent in the garden, subtract from God's Word to offer us competing promises for our joy, encouraging us to take whatever "fruit" we want because we "will certainly not die." Satan also uses false teachers to add to God's Word—"God said we can't even touch the tree." Going beyond God's Word in this way leads to legalism.

Are you familiar with the term *legalism*? What does it mean, and how does this problem work its way into our lives?

How does legalism rob us of joy in Christ?

Legalism places the focus of the Christian life on what you can do for God instead of what God has done for you in Christ. In the first century, a group called the Judaizers infiltrated the church and taught that to be a Christian you must continue to follow the Jewish law that was fulfilled in Christ. However, the whole point of the gospel is that we cannot meet God's standard and need Jesus to do it for us. Legalism robs us of joy because it places an impossible standard before us.

What does Paul's list in Phlippians 3:4-6 show about where he had placed his delight and trust before knowing Christ?

Paul knew the dangers of legalism—he was a recovering legalist. Notice that in his résumé there is not one mention of God, just a list of things Paul did for God. On the road to Damascus, though, Paul found out that what God has done for us is far more important than anything we can do for God. Rituals, race, religion, rules, and reputation do not save. Only Jesus saves.

||| *The rallying cry of legalism is "Yes, Christ, but also . . . "* |||

Read Philippians 3:7-9. What became more valuable to Paul than any accomplishment he had ever achieved?

Paul missed the joy of knowing Jesus because of misplaced priorities. How do we recognize misplaced priorities in our own lives?

The word *surpassing* means "of exceptional value." Jesus is more valuable than we could ever imagine. We need Him desperately. The joy He offers surpasses any reputation or accomplishment. Paul came to see that Jesus is like the treasure buried in a field that we should sell everything to possess (Matthew 13:44). When we find that we have elevated anyone or anything higher than Jesus, our priorities have been misplaced and our joy is incomplete.

Where does true righteousness come from? Why is this better than a righteousness that comes from our own doing?

What assurance does grace free of legalism give us when we miss the mark before God?

True righteousness has only ever been achieved once, in Jesus Christ. Everyone else the Bible calls righteous is only righteous because of the faith he or she has placed in God, whereby He accounts Jesus's righteousness as his or her own. The legalist becomes afraid when he or she misses the mark and fall into sin. Those whose righteousness is in Christ mourn their sin, but they are not fearful because Christ's perfect righteousness stands on their behalf. Only when we know Christ and boast in Christ, do we have real hope.

Compared to Christ, how should we consider anything else we are tempted to take confidence in (such as goodness, ethnicity, baptism, church attendance, or politics)?

How do we get to the place where our confidence is in Christ alone?

A right understanding of the gospel values Jesus above all things.

Read Philippians 3:10-11. How does freely-given grace encourage us to know Christ at deeper and deeper levels?

Practically speaking, what does it look like when we make it our goal "to know him and the power of his resurrection and the fellowship of his sufferings, being conformed to his death" (v. 10)?

Grace gives us freedom in our relationship with God. We don't approach Him as children who have disappointed Him, but as children He loves and is glad to see. Trust is built as we strengthen our relationship with Him. We do this by spending time in our Bibles and in worship, talking with God in prayer, and building our trust in Him through our relationship with Jesus and His followers. And as we do this—as we learn to rejoice in the Lord and boast in all God is and does for us in Christ—we will be willing to follow Jesus into suffering and death because we know that what awaits us is resurrection and glory.

DOXOLOGY

WRITE IT DOWN

Committing our joy in the Lord to the page is, as Paul said, no trouble and a safeguard. In light of this truth, personalize Philippians 3:1-11 by listing the reasons you are tempted to place confidence in the flesh and the reasons you have for placing your confidence solely in Christ.

Reasons for confidence in the flesh	Reasons for confidence in Christ alone

HIDE IT IN YOUR HEART

As a way to help keep these two lists in right perspective, memorize Philippians 3:8.

More than that, I also consider everything to be a loss in view of the surpassing value of knowing Christ Jesus my Lord. Because of him I have suffered the loss of all things and consider them as dung, so that I may gain Christ.

PHILIPPIANS 3:8

DISCIPLESHIP

Ask God to help you identify some false teachers and false teachings that might be influencing you. List them here.

Now, rate your typical level of concern over those false teachings. Do you tend to think of those influences in your life as "evil" (Philippians 3:2) or as "not a big deal"? Based on this week's study, what correlation is there between your answer and the joy you are able to experience in the Lord?

Knowing Christ was more valuable to Paul than anything else. What ideas, fears, or pursuits tend to keep this from being true in your life?

What practices do you need to implement or continue so that you better understand those ideas, fears, or pursuits correctly—as false teachings that Satan wants to use to steal your joy?

Session Six

The Joy of
STANDING FIRM

GROUP STUDY

Welcome everyone to the group. Take a few minutes to
review session 5 before starting session 6.

Before starting the new content each week, we'll take a few minutes to review the personal study from the previous week.

DOCTRINE. What is one key belief/conviction that arose from the text?

DOXOLOGY. What is one way you can respond to that belief/conviction in worship?

DISCIPLESHIP. How is the text leading you to act differently going forward?

Philippians 3:1-11 assures us of this: knowing Christ is an internal joy that does not exist apart from the external effect of battling any temptation toward false teachings. That battle against distortions of the gospel will continue until Christ returns. With that battle in view, this week we'll be encouraged by the joy of standing firm.

To prepare for video session 6, pray that God will help
each person understand and apply this truth:

To stand firm in the faith until we cross the finish line, we must imitate those who live with a heavenly mindset.

WATCH

Use this space to take notes during the video teaching.

DRAMA

Use the following questions and prompts to guide
your discussion of the video teaching.

What is a goal you have had (or have now) that you've pressed on toward despite difficulty?

Why is that goal worth the effort it takes to endure?

Read Philippians 3:12-16.

What was Paul's primary goal to pursue each and every day?

Paul stood firm in his pursuit of knowing and following Christ as he longed for his future day of resurrection. The steadfast pursuit of Christ made Paul's earthly life extremely difficult (See 2 Corinthians 11:23-28).

Considering this, how do you react to Paul's call to think in the same way he did?

What keeps us from forgetting everything else to press forward in utter faithfulness to Christ?

Read Philippians 3:17-21.

Share about someone you've wanted to imitate in order to achieve a certain goal. How did the imitation help you?

How does this help you understand why Paul's instruction to imitate him isn't prideful but loving?

Who is someone whose faith you watch and attempt to imitate? How has that person helped you know the joy of standing firm?

.

Do you aspire to be a model Christian? If so, how so? If not, why not?

In the video teaching, Juan highlighted two reasons the text teaches that we are to imitate those who are running well:

1. If you're imitating those who are running poorly, their end is destruction (v. 18-19).
2. Our citizenship is in heaven (v. 20-21).

What is our standard for determining who is running poorly and those who are running well?

How should the reality of the future impact the reality of present goals and decisions?

What remaining questions or comments do you have about this session's teaching video? What was challenging, convicting, encouraging, or timely for your current circumstances?

CLOSE IN PRAYER.
Prayer Requests:

DOCTRINE

We left off in last week's reading with Paul expressing his highest goal in life—to know Christ. This pursuit brought him a joy that surpassed any other in its value. Ironically, that joy was expressed to him both in Christ's power and suffering. And Paul's suffering was excessive. At this point in the letter, the Philippian believers might have thought Paul's Christlike attitude, while admirable, was too far beyond what was possible for ordinary Christians like them. We might find ourselves thinking that, too.

Read Philippians 3:12-14. Why did Paul feel the need to point out that he wasn't yet "perfect"?

In your own words, what did Paul do to continue knowing and becoming more like Christ?

Notice the language Paul used here—"make every effort," "take hold," "reaching forward," and "pursue." What does this indicate about the goal of knowing Christ?

When would Paul's goal be realized? When will you fully know Christ and be made perfectly sinless like Him?

Knowing Christ is a strenuous, continuous, lifelong pursuit; it is a marathon, not a sprint.

"One thing I do: Forgetting what is behind and reaching forward to what is ahead" (v. 13b) is a commonly quoted verse. However, it is often misapplied. Though it may be temporarily useful to forget whatever negative thing happened yesterday and set your sights on whatever positive thing you hope will happen tomorrow, Paul's meaning was far greater than this.

Identify what Paul meant by "what is ahead" (v. 14).

What was "behind" Paul that he had determined to forget?

How do we run this race in order to be conformed to the image of Christ? We fix our eyes on the promise of being raised to eternal life in perfect communion with Jesus. We take our eyes off our past victories, failures, and disappointments and seek to be conformed into that image even now, here on earth. Knowing Christ in this way requires knowledge, but not merely intellectual or theological knowledge. Knowing Christ requires the application of knowledge so that it transforms us into His image. As we follow Jesus's steps in God's power by faith, we become more and more like Christ. And one day, we will be perfectly conformed to Christ, but that day is not yet.

Read Philippians 3:15-16. What does Paul mean when he says we "should live up to whatever truth we have attained"?

Living up to the truth we have attained is a call to stay in the race, refusing to look back. It's Paul's call to progress in the Christian life, keeping your eyes focused on the finish line. Sure the race may become hard. There will be hurdles along the way, but you can be certain you will win the prize! Not because of your ability to run well, but because Christ has already run the race and won the prize for you. And there are other believers who serve as an example for you.

Read Philippians 3:17-19. Why do we need to "pay careful attention to those who live according to the example" we have in Scripture?

What connection is there between verse 17 and verse 16, the imitation of faithful believers and living up to the truth we have attained?

As Paul made clear in verses 2-3, the Philippians needed to watch out because they would be tempted to imitate the wrong people. Instead, Paul invited them to imitate him—to look at the way that he followed Christ so that they might have a faithful example. The examples of false teachers would only lead them into sadness. The example of Paul and others like him (2:19-30) would lead them into joy.

Put verse 19 in your own words.

What can we know is true about people who live as enemies of the cross of Christ?

What happens to those who follow those poor examples and do not stand firm in faith?

> *Who you imitate is who you'll end up
> looking like and sounding like.*

In contrast to the description Paul gives in verse 19 of enemies of the cross of Christ, what does Jesus call us to, instead? What do the following verses teach us are repeatable qualities we should demonstrate?

John 5:24

Galatians 5:24

2 Corinthians 10:17-18

Colossians 3:1-2

It is not only people we imitate. We will imitate whatever voice it is we give our attention to, whether in a face-to-face relationship or in reading, watching a screen, or listening to a podcast. If we give our attention to the earthly-minded, we are also headed for destruction unless we repent. If we give our attention to God's Word and those who imitate the kingdom values it teaches, we show that our citizenship is in heaven.

Read Philippians 3:20-21. Why was it important for Paul to remind these believers of their citizenship?

Philippi was a Roman colony. The Philippians, as a society, were proud of the Roman government and their Roman citizenship. However, Paul pointed the Philippian Christians away from their earthly political allegiance to their heavenly one. He knew that when given priority, allegiance to our earthly citizenship always gets in the way of living for God's kingdom values.

How does our view of eternity inform our lives here and now?

We are strangers on this earth, but we live here reflecting heaven's priorities.

Does that mean we shouldn't care about the things of this earth, like politics, culture, sports, and so forth? What does it mean?

We are called to be faithful in the here and now. Many things we celebrate and pursue are good things, but they are not ultimate things. The things of this earth are passing away. We can enjoy them without selling out to them. Instead, we eagerly await a Savior who will come from heaven again. On that day, we all will give an account. That day will also be a day of transformation for those who are found in Christ. The Lord Jesus will transform our bodies into a glorious body like His—raised from the dead by the power of God, no longer to battle sin and temptation nor to struggle, suffer, or die.

> *Since all these glories are true for us who believe, why would we set our minds on earthly things that are passing away?*

Read Philippians 4:1. What continued example does Paul give in the way he addresses believers in this verse?

Based on the example Paul gave, how would you summarize the "manner" in which we should stand firm in the Lord?

The family of faith is an inheritance from the Lord. Standing firm in the faith is the crown jewel. You are the joy and crown of those who set an example for you in Christ. It is a calling and a great responsibility. But to endure faithfully, you must stand firm, imitating those believers who have a heavenly mindset.

DOXOLOGY

WRITE IT DOWN

As a way of identifying how you can joyfully stand firm and reach forward to the heavenly goal, personally apply Paul's words in the second half of Philippians 3:13.

What past victories, failures, and disappointments are behind me?

What is ahead for me in Christ Jesus?

CALL UPON GOD

Thank God for the promise of Christ's return to finally and forever establish your heavenly citizenship.

Review your list of past victories, failures, and disappointments, acknowledging that you need to leave them behind.

Ask God to help you focus on those promises ahead for you in Christ Jesus, and invite Him to reveal them to you anytime you think differently.

By name, thank Him for the people He has put in your life who set before you an example of kingdom mindedness to follow.

Commit to joyfully stand firm in Christ until the last day.

DISCIPLESHIP

What goals are you determined to accomplish in life? How do they compare to the goals with which Paul pressed forward?

How would you summarize the truth you have attained to this point regarding the goal of your life in Christ?

Who are some people you know who genuinely seek to live faithfully according to God's Word?

What would change in your life this week if you were to imitate their example?

Session Seven

The Joy of
COMMUNION
with GOD

GROUP STUDY

START

Welcome everyone to the group. Take a few minutes to
review session 6 before starting session 7.

Before starting the new content each week, we'll take a few minutes to review the personal
study from the previous week.

DOCTRINE. What is one key belief/conviction that arose from the text?

DOXOLOGY. What is one way you can respond to that belief/conviction in worship?

DISCIPLESHIP. How is the text leading you to act differently going forward?

One major emphasis about joy in Paul's letter to the Philippians is that we need to imitate
others who walk in that joy. The experience of true joy is uncommon. The more common
experience in gospel partnerships, in living and dying as we seek to know the Lord, in
humble obedience, and in standing firm through life's trials, is a sense of lack that manifests
itself in frustration and complaining. So we desperately need to pay attention to those who
serve as uncommon examples and imitate them. This week we're going to see how those
examples can help us experience the joy of communion with God.

To prepare for video session 7, pray that God will help
each person understand and apply this truth:

*Believing the promise of God's presence empowers
us to dwell on all that is excellent, that we might
live life in a manner worthy of the gospel.*

WATCH

Use this space to take notes during the video teaching.

DRAMA

"The Rule of Seven" is a longtime marketing principle stating that people need to "see" a message seven times before they will act on it. Obviously, some of us rush to action more quickly and others of us who are distracted require additional reminders, but the general point is clear: it takes reiteration for a message to sink in.

What about you? What helps a message really sink in for you?

What is the connection between "The Rule of Seven" and Paul's words in Philippians 4:9 to "do what you have learned and received and heard from me, and seen in me"?

Have you ever been told, "Do as I say, not as I do"? Or, if you're a parent, maybe you've said those words yourself! Why isn't "do as I say, not as I do" an effective parenting strategy?

What are some specific ways God's commands have been and are now effectively reiterated to you?

Looking at the rest of verse 9, what promise is there for those who let those reminders lead them to personal action?

Does this seem strange to you? Why is it that applying Paul's life message results in the experience of God's peace-giving presence?

In the video teaching, Juan pointed out that these are anchor thoughts here in verse 9 because they help us connect what comes before and after it. Today we're discussing what comes before verse 9, and next week we will take a look at the conclusion of Paul's letter to the Philippians in the verses that follow.

Read Philippians 4:2-8.

Paul follows up his mention of the conflict between Euodia and Syntyche with rejoicing and graciousness, along with a statement of fact: "The Lord is near" (v. 5). What relevance should the Lord's nearness have in the way believers relate to one another in disagreements?

As the Philippian believers struggled to rejoice and be gracious in their relationships with one another, what did Paul remind them to do (v. 6)? What effect does prayer have over all our worries (v. 7)? Why?

As we long for peace in the worrisome situations we face, what does verse 8 instruct us to do, as a partner to prayer (v. 6) and imitation (v. 9)? How is this possible in a world where technology makes an abundance of false teachings seem more near than that which is "morally excellent" and "praiseworthy"?

Juan explained that the greatest promise in all of Scripture is the promise of God's peace-filled presence.

Is it possible for us to experience that promise even now, this side of heaven? Are you experiencing that promise now? Explain.

What remaining questions or comments do you have about this session's teaching video? What was challenging, convicting, encouraging, or timely for your current circumstances?

CLOSE IN PRAYER.

Prayer Requests:

DOCTRINE

Think back to the last time you had a major conflict with someone. Who was it with? What was it about? Have you resolved it? In our first week of study, we learned there is joy in gospel partnerships. But what happens when those partnerships become marked by conflict? Does a lack of joyful community among believers steal the joy of living and dying for Christ, the joy of humility, the joy of obedience, the joy of knowing Christ, and the joy of standing firm? Does our disunity impact the extent of our joyful communion with God?

Read Philippians 4:1-3. Why would Paul publicly call out these two women right after expressing his deep love for them and encouragement to stand firm?

The issue of these believers' reconciliation was urgent, but Paul doesn't identify the reason for their disagreement. What does the nonmention of the nature of their conflict teach us about what matters most?

Euodia and Syntyche were mature believers. The two women labored side by side with Paul and others in the gospel. Their Christian faith was evident—their "names are in the book of life" (v. 3). Their faith had been worth imitating, and then conflict between them was manifesting itself in a way that needed correction before it divided the community of faith. This is why Paul makes no mention of their actual disagreement—the source of their conflict mattered far less than the effect of their conflict. For the sake of communion with God and His church, agreement between them was urgent.

> *If we are to experience the fullness of joy in communion with God, we must keep the main thing the main thing—the gospel!*

Paul calls on the community of faith to help each other maintain Christian unity. Based on his example in Philippians 4:1-3, what does that mean? Mark each answer that applies.

☐ advocate for reconciliation

☐ assume motives

☐ take sides

☐ pray for unity

☐ help out

☐ think the best of each other

☐ look for evidences of God's grace

☐ gossip about it

☐ stick your nose in everyone's business

☐ get involved in the life of the church

☐ love people

The fact is, our joy of communion with God will face opposition both externally and internally. We must resolve, then, to rejoice in all circumstances, show graciousness to all people, and not be anxious about anything.

Read Philippians 4:4-7. Does the command to "Rejoice!" seem out of place to you in the context of a churchwide conversation about conflict? Why?

Where was the Philippians' joy meant to be rooted? Based on Paul's urging in verses 2-3, where were they likely rooting their joy instead?

What about Paul's life and circumstance makes his command in verse 6 legitimately repeatable ("Do as I say and as I do")?

Paul was in prison when he wrote this letter, and it was in that very circumstance that he exclaimed, "Rejoice!" This wasn't a onetime, brief moment of emotional relief. In Acts 16, Paul and Silas sang hymns in prison! Joy marked Paul's life—all the time. When we root our joy in the Lord—who He is and what He has done—we can rejoice in the face of every circumstance.

Read James 1:2-4. Why can we rejoice in all circumstances?

Paul extended the call more broadly in Philippians 4:5, saying we must show graciousness to everyone—rude and cranky people, obnoxious non-Christians, and even hateful anti-Christians. When someone breaks up with you or your spouse forgets your birthday, be gracious. When a driver cuts you off in traffic or your employer is overly demanding, be gracious. When the business deal goes south or your teacher gives you a failing grade, be gracious. Every situation, every encounter is an opportunity to show gentleness, the gentleness of Christ, to all people—because the Lord is near.

What did Paul mean by "The Lord is near"? In what sense is the Lord near to believers?

What if we don't sense His nearness when we are dealing with rude people? What help in verse 6 does Paul's example give us to imitate?

What promise is there for those who faithfully turn to God in prayer regarding interpersonal conflict, graciousness in difficult situations, and worrisome problems?

In every type of circumstance, the Lord is at work drawing us into deeper communion with Him.

As Paul brought his letter to a close, he urged the Philippians to let their minds dwell on all that is excellent and to practice all that they have heard and seen in him, in order that they may experience the presence of God.

Read Philippians 4:8. What is the essence of this command?

Paul commands us to take careful responsibility for what we allow into our minds. "Dwell on these things" indicates a habit of thought. When we come to faith in Christ, we are forever united with Him. Nothing can separate us from the love God has for us in Christ. That is, nothing can harm, endanger, or sever our union with God. However, letting our minds dwell on earthly things that lead us to sin harms, endangers, and breaks our communion, or fellowship, with God. So we must dwell on the excellent things of God. The list Paul gave in verse 8 describes the nature of Jesus's thought life when He walked upon the earth.

Record what the following verses teach about our thought lives:

> **Luke 6:45**
>
> **Romans 12:2**
>
> **2 Corinthians 10:5**
>
> **Colossians 3:2**
>
> **1 Peter 1:13**

What are some clear and present dangers to the thought lives of followers of Jesus?

We are accountable for our thoughts and have the ability to limit, manage, shape, and pattern them. Learning to do this is a part of the process of growing in Christlikeness and living in the joy of communion with God.

Read Romans 8:5-9. Paul joins together our actions with our thought life in starkly contrasting choices. Is there a middle ground? Can we watch, listen to, and read whatever we want according to the flesh and also live in communion with God? Why or why not?

| | | | *Our doing flows out of our thinking.* | | | |

Paul summed up his instructions to the Philippians by telling them to recall the teaching and example that he gave them personally. They were to lean on this example and teaching to continue forward in their growth.

What gave Paul the authority and credibility to call others to imitate him?

Discipleship was a prevalent part of the culture of ancient Israel. Not only that, but discipleship was also the clear commission of Jesus. We know Paul took seriously the task of making disciples because we see him practicing it and instructing others to do it. For example, in 2 Timothy 2:2 he explicitly told Timothy to teach faithful men who would teach others. In Philippians 4:9 Paul gave a brief overview of the discipleship process.

What are some of the elements of discipleship seen in Philippians 4:9?

How do these elements of discipleship relate to the joy of communion with God?

DOXOLOGY

PRAYERFULLY EXAMINE YOURSELF

In Philippians 4:8, Paul listed eight adjectives that serve as a sort of filter by which you can evaluate the benefit of something to your thought life. Invite God to help you examine each one individually. Jot down any thoughts He brings to mind, then prayerfully answer the questions below.

1. TRUE—not false or deceptive

2. HONORABLE—revered, venerated

3. JUST—that which is right, correct

4. PURE—clean, unstained, spotless, uncontaminated

5. LOVELY—pleasing, winsome

6. COMMENDABLE—held in high esteem, has a good name

7. EXCELLENT—of high quality

8. PRAISEWORTHY—deserving of recognition

What keeps you from thinking on these things?

What helps you think on these things?

How would thinking on these things increase your communion with God?

DISCIPLESHIP

Look again at the ways we are called to help each other maintain Christian unity (page 100). In which of these do you need to engage more deeply? Explain.

Which of these commands is hardest for you to follow: rejoice in the Lord always (v. 4), let your graciousness be known to everyone (v. 5), or don't worry about anything but pray about everything (v. 6)? Specifically, what is the Lord calling you to do to improve in that area?

Who in your life needs a model of joy in communion with God, even in difficult circumstances? What are some practical ways you can be that example?

Where do you need to refocus your thought life so that you can delight in communion with the God of peace? How will you do that?

Session Eight

The Joy of
GENEROSITY

GROUP STUDY

Welcome everyone to the group. Take a few minutes to
review session 7 before starting session 8.

Before starting the new content each week, we'll take a few minutes to review the personal study from the previous week.

DOCTRINE. What is one key belief/conviction that arose from the text?

DOXOLOGY. What is one way you can respond to that belief/conviction in worship?

DISCIPLESHIP. How is the text leading you to act differently going forward?

Reviewing these previous studies together each week has helped us set the context for the current week's story, readying us for discussion of new truths. It has also provided account-ability for us to put into practice the things we are learning. This will continue to be true for each of us now that this particular group study is coming to an end. This week we're going to examine the joy of generosity.

Why will it be important for you to continue to "review" the truths God has taught you in this study going forward? How will you do that?

To prepare for video session 8, pray that God will help
each person understand and apply this truth:

||| *When we believe God is faithful, we will give generously.* |||

WATCH

Use this space to take notes during the video teaching.

DRAMA

Use these questions to discuss the video teaching.

Why is it uncomfortable for many of us to talk about money? Why should we talk about it despite our discomfort?

The Bible teaches about money and possessions in many places. What are some of the truths about money you have learned from the Scriptures?

Read Philippians 4:10-13.

Philippians 4:13 is a well-loved but often misunderstood verse. Considering the context of the Philippians' generous giving, what did Paul mean when he wrote, "I am able to do all things through him who strengthens me"?

Juan explained that contentment is "a really important secret that affects our generosity." What are the people, things, or circumstances we tend to look to for contentment?

Why do we struggle to trust God to provide for us?

Many people believe and say they trust God completely, yet struggle with contentment. They do not make joyful and generous giving a regular practice, because they are worried about the future and believe they must work, first and foremost, to provide for that future. Do you see the connection? Discontentment comes when full trust in the Lord is displaced.

Why is it so easy to get caught up in the material stuff of this world? How can we guard against that?

Why is it impossible to trust God's provision and not be generous?

Read Philippians 4:14-23.

Have you ever thought of financial sacrifice as something joyful? Explain.

In the video teaching, Juan highlighted four teachings from the text that express why we are to joyfully give:

1. When we give generously, the Lord cares for His workers through our generosity (vv. 10-16).
2. When we give generously, we receive a return on our investment (v. 17).
3. When we give generously, it pleases the Lord (v. 18).
4. When we give generously, we glorify God (vv. 19-20).

Do any of these reasons stand out to you, either as a point of confusion, personal testimony, challenge, or encouragement? Explain.

What remaining questions or comments do you have about this session's teaching video? What was challenging, convicting, encouraging, or timely for your current circumstances?

As was pointed out in the beginning of today's lesson, meeting with Christian friends to talk about what God is teaching us is vitally important to continued spiritual growth. It doesn't have to happen in a group study like this—it can happen over coffee or lunch, on a walk, or even in the break room at work! No matter where or when it happens, it will ready us to receive the truths God has for us and will provide accountability to walk in those truths.

CLOSE IN PRAYER.

Prayer Requests:

DOCTRINE

Read Philippians 4:9-10. As Paul expressed his desire for the Philippians to put into practice his teaching and example of gospel living, what recent example of that kind of gospel living came to mind?

Since money is one of the topics most people don't like to discuss, it might have been risky for Paul to save these words for the end of his letter. He had received a financial gift from the Philippians, and he wanted to talk about it. Some of the Philippians might have started to doze off or head out for lunch when chapter 4 verse 10 was first read aloud. But Paul wasn't bringing up the topic because he wanted to make things awkward at church that day; he wanted believers to experience the joy of generosity.

Read Philippians 4:11-14. Why did Paul feel the need to clarify his reason for joy?

What did Paul want to guard against in his own life and in the lives of other believers? Record what the following verses teach you:

1 Timothy 6:6-10

Colossians 3:5-6

Hebrews 13:5-6

Ephesians 5:5-6

Paul did not expect the financial gift, and he was not trying to squeeze more out of them. He was joyful for the gift, but he would not base his joy on whether or not he received such gifts because God's Word cautions us against that. Covetousness is idolatry because it seeks joy and satisfaction in something we don't have, something God has not given us, instead of in Him. We find our ultimate joy and satisfaction in God and God alone.

What do Paul's words in verses 11 and 12 teach us about any discontentment and lack of joy in the Lord we may experience in life?

How do experiences of abundance teach us to be content? Read James 1:16-17 for help.

How do experiences of circumstantial need teach us to be content? Read 2 Corinthians 12:9-10 for help.

Contentment is learned, and God does not waste any circumstance to teach us that lesson. For Paul, God used both hunger and delicious meals to remind him that God provides. He had used both financial hardship and generous financial gifts in Paul's life to affirm Paul's need for God alone.

Based on verse 13, what else had God taught Paul through those life experiences?

Considering the aim and focus of Paul's life as expressed throughout this letter, what kinds of things do you think Paul meant that God's strength would allow him to do?

Philippians 4:13 is not a verse about scoring touchdowns and winning championships. The secret of contentment—of joyful living—is living for the Lord in the strength of the Lord. It is learning to rely on His strength to carry out His purposes in all situations, in every circumstance. Sometimes we must rely on His strength as we enjoy times of abundance, and sometimes we must rely on His strength as we experience times of need. And all the time, He is faithful to provide for our need.

What is the relationship between contentment and generous giving?

Read Philippians 4:15-19. What "profit" was Paul seeking in the generosity of these believers?

The word *profit* is literally "fruit." He was not seeking his own financial gain, nor did he mean that they could expect God to reward them financially for their giving. But the fact was, they would all indeed "profit" from those gifts. In another passage on giving (2 Corinthians 9:10-13), Paul listed some of the non-monetary rewards we may receive for supporting the ministry of others.

How does giving to help others, even out of our own need, stretch and deepen our faith?

What benefits do we receive when we share financially in the ministry of others?

In verse 18, how did Paul describe the financial gift the Philippians had sent? What does this language teach us about our generous giving?

The generous gift of the Philippians was an act of worship. In the Old Testament, the people's pleasing sacrifices met the needs of God's priests. In the New Testament, we learn that we are God's temple and His holy priests who offer spiritual sacrifices to God through Jesus Christ (1 Peter 2:5). Our whole lives are to be living sacrifices to God (Romans 12:1). This lifestyle of worship certainly includes our finances!

When we consider that it is an act of worship, how do the following verses help you see why financial giving necessitates joyful generosity?

Psalm 95:1-6

Matthew 4:10

2 Corinthians 1:3-4

Romans 11:36

Matthew 2:11

John 3:16

From Philippians 4:19, what can we know God will do for us when we worship Him through joyful generosity?

This is not a name it, claim it promise of prosperity; this is a promise that God will care for His children. The Philippians did not give out of abundance. They were truly poor, and Paul wanted to reassure them that in their generosity, God would supply all that they needed. In fact, He already had.

God has given us His greatest treasure in Christ Jesus, who received God's wrath in our place in order that we would receive forgiveness for sin. Jesus is our ultimate provision; beyond Him, we truly need nothing else.

Read Philippians 4:20-23. What does verse 20 teach us was Paul's greatest aim?

|| *Our generous giving glorifies God as the faithful caretaker of His people.* ||

What does verse 23 teach us was Paul's greatest hope for the Philippian believers?

Ultimately, the reason for everything Paul did and taught others to do—engaging in gospel partnerships, living and dying for Christ, seeking to know Christ and respond to Him in humble gratitude, standing firm, communing with God, and giving generously—was to glorify God. With that purpose in view, Paul ended as he had begun (1:2): with a prayer that Christ's grace would be with their spirit. This was a reminder that they were to be united in the joy of the Lord—in every circumstance.

DOXOLOGY

WRITE IT DOWN

Philippians 4 teaches us that gospel contentment compels joyful generosity. On the other hand, if you are not fully content in God alone, then you likely covet something, and that something will prohibit joyful generosity. Complete this sentence to identify your tempting thoughts toward covetousness:

If only _____ **,**
then I would be content.

What does your answer reveal about your level of contentment in God?

CALL ON GOD

Thank God for providing so generously the greatest provision you need—salvation in Jesus Christ. As you recognize those areas of life where you fail to trust Him completely to continue providing what you need, ask for His help. Invite Him to give you the strength to view and generously share your finances as an opportunity to display His glory.

HIDE IT IN YOUR HEART

As a way of remembering to live a lifestyle that demonstrates joy in generosity in every circumstance, memorize Philippians 4:19-20.

And my God will supply all your needs according to
his riches in glory in Christ Jesus. Now to our God
and Father be glory forever and ever. Amen.

PHILIPPIANS 4:19-20

DISCIPLESHIP

In what situations do you find it hard to experience contentment?

What does Philippians 4:10-23 encourage you to do about that?

What perspective on your finances do you need to take to truly live a joyfully generous life?

Under what circumstance(s) do you need to appropriate the promise of God's abundant provision (v. 19) for yourself today? What steps can you take to set aside your fear or discontentment to walk in that promise?

If only Solomon had written a book on wisdom.

Oh, wait.

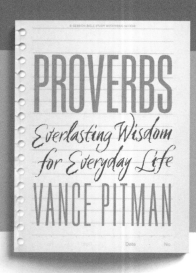

Take a month-long journey through all 31 chapters of Proverbs. You'll not only gain an appreciation for this popular and applicable book of the Bible, you'll also begin to develop a daily habit of seeking wisdom from God's Word. In addition to the four session videos, you get access to 31 short, daily teaching videos (one for each chapter), all included in the purchase price of the *Bible Study Book*.

Learn more online or call 800.458.2772.
lifeway.com/proverbs

Lifeway

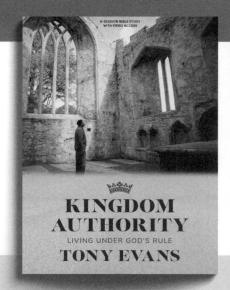

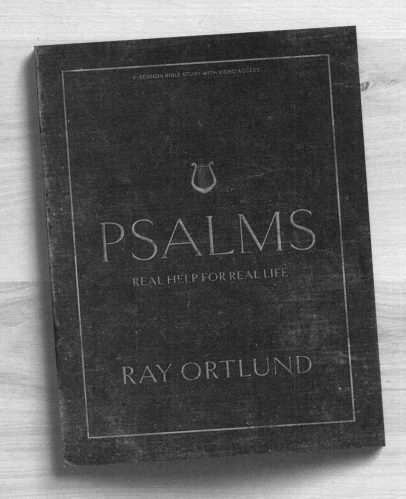

Learn to find help for all of life's circumstances.

The Psalms are filled with people venting surprisingly honest feelings toward God, whether it be anger, disappointment, awe, or happiness. This new study from Ray Ortlund will help you see that the Psalms are a place that God has provided to encounter Him and find help, rest, hope, courage, joy, and confidence for whatever you face in life.

Get the most from your study.

Are you ready to gain understanding and wisdom from the book of Philippians and discover the joy of partnership when it's for the sake of the gospel?

In this study, you'll learn to:

- Rejoice in the Lord in every circumstance
- Walk in humility
- Discover purpose and joy
- Treasure Christ above all else
- Pray with thanksgiving and gratitude

STUDYING ON YOUR OWN?

Watch the teaching sessions, available via redemption code for individual video-streaming access, printed in this *Bible Study Book*.

LEADING A GROUP?

Each group member will need a *Philippians Bible Study Book*, which includes access to teaching videos. Because all participants will have access to the video content, you can choose to watch the videos outside of your group meeting if desired. Or, if you're watching together and someone misses a group meeting, they'll have the flexibility to catch up.

ADDITIONAL RESOURCES

eBOOK
Includes the content of this printed book but offers the convenience and flexibility that come with mobile technology.

005840910 **$19.99**

More *Philippians* resources can be found online at lifeway.com/studyphilippians